My Backyard Is for the Birds: A Guide to the Most Common Northeastern Birds for the Young Backyard Birdwatcher

My Backyard Is for the Birds: A Guide to the Most Common Northeastern Birds for the Young Backyard Birdwatcher

By Jennifer Scardino

Illustrated by Karen Padula

RoseDog ❧ Books

PITTSBURGH, PENNSYLVANIA 15222

RoseDog Books
701 Smithfield Street
Pittsburgh, PA 15222
Visit our website at *www.rosedogbookstore.com*

ISBN: 978-1-4349-3222-8
eISBN: 978-1-4349-3289-1

My Backyard Is for the Birds: A Guide to the Most Common Northeastern Birds for the Young Backyard Birdwatcher

By Jennifer Scardino

Illustrated by Karen Padula

As a little girl, my grandparents shared with me their love of birds. We all would scurry to the back door to see the "accidental" bird that would occasionally pass through the yard on some invisible migration trail. I was learning something valuable: I was learning to appreciate nature.

Everyday, wherever you go, nature is living, working, and playing, just like you and me. Bird watching is one of the simple things in life many people are too busy, too young or too cool to enjoy. Yet it's virtually free and so relaxing you might just fall asleep doing it, as I have many times.

Bird appreciation should begin with children. In so doing, they will spend more time outdoors. They will also be more proactive in protecting wildlife from danger and extinction. Children can join the effort to provide safe havens and food for migrating birds facing long journeys, cold winters, and barren, dry summers. But most of all, children will gain a greater appreciation for God and his creation.

I find myself some twenty years older, on my lawn chair in the backyard or looking out my window, watching the antics of my backyard birds. I have trudged through shin-deep snow and blowing wind to feed "my" birds, all the while having sweet memories of my grandparents because I know they did the very same thing!

I hope this book inspires you to look out your window to see what birds you might have and to share them with the little person in your life.

This guide contains birds most commonly found in the Northeast area of the United States. It is not meant to be exhaustive but rather a beginner's guide to get a young person interested in the joy of bird watching.

CARDINAL

COLOR: The male is red with a black mask around his face. The female is greenish tan with an orange beak. They both have a big, fluffy point on the top of their heads.

EAT: They prefer to eat sunflower seeds.

APPEARANCE: They will rarely land on a hanging bird feeder. You can see them on the ground underneath your feeder. Cardinals like to stick together. If you see the male first, the female is usually not far away. Cardinals are very shy, so you must watch them from afar.

GOLDFINCHES

COLOR: In summer the male is a beautiful bright yellow with black on the very top of his head and a black tail and wings. In winter they lose their bright color and turn a dull yellow, which makes them look very much like the female.

The female is not as lovely. She is a dull yellow with a slightly brighter belly. Her color changes very little in the winter.

EAT: Goldfinches will eat sunflower seed and/or Nyjer (thistle) seed.

APPEARANCE: You can have fun with goldfinches. They are very acrobatic. For instance, you can go to any garden center and buy a thistle feeder that has holes below the perch and this forces the goldfinch to hang upside down to eat!

BLACKCAP CHICKADEE

COLOR: Their name can help you remember what they look like. Both males and females have a black patch on their head and throat.

EAT: They will eat almost any seed you give them.

APPEARANCE: These birds are great! They are probably the bravest of all the backyard birds you will ever have in your yard. Because chickadees aren't shy, with a little patience you can have them eating sunflower seeds right out of your hand. They are also chatterboxes and will talk to you when you are in the yard together.

TUFTED TITMOUSE

COLOR: These birds are related to the chickadee, and again their name will help you identify them. These small birds have a fluffy point on the top of their heads (much like a cardinal). They have grey on their back and are mostly white on their belly.

EAT: Titmice prefer sunflower seed. Unlike the chickadee, this sweet bird is shy and will not usually eat from your hand.

APPEARANCE: They too are big noisemakers with no manners. Titmice will always yell at you and chatter away with their friends while their mouths are full!

WHITE-BREASTED NUTHATCH

COLOR: Nuthatches are bright bluish grey with a white belly. The male has a black patch on top of his head. The female does not have this black patch on her head. A unique feature of the nuthatch is their stubby tail. It almost looks as though someone trimmed it too short!

EAT: These interesting birds love sunflowers too, but they don't stick around the feeder very long. They creep down the tree, grab a seed, and fly back into the tree. Once there, they wedge the seed into a piece of bark and with their very strong beaks they open the seed and get the yummy pulp inside.

APPEARANCE: Nuthatches are wonderful to watch. They have very strong feet that allow them to cling tightly to trees; because of this, they are able to hop up and down trees headfirst! Nuthatches are nervous nellies, so watch from a distance and be extra quiet.

AMERICAN ROBIN

COLOR: They all have a brownish black back with a rusty red belly.

EAT: You don't need to have any feeder at all to have a robin in your yard. In fact, they don't even like feeders. They prefer worms. (Ick!)

APPEARANCE: You will most likely see a robin after you water your lawn or after a good rain. They hop around poking holes in the ground, tasting for juicy fat worms. They love to splash around in birdbaths too. Because robins go to warmer temperatures for winter, their return is often the first sign that spring has once again arrived.

BLUE JAY

COLOR: The blue jay has a beautiful bright blue back and tail with a white belly and a black ring around its neck.

EAT: Everything! These guys are not picky eaters. They also eat fast, as if they haven't eaten in days.

APPEARANCE: Usually when a robin enters your bird-feeding area, all of the other birds will scurry away and wait patiently until he/she leaves. I like to call them the bullies of the bird world. They can be very mean to other birds and make a lot of noise!

DOVE or MOURNING DOVE

COLOR: Both males and females are brownish grey in color. They look much like the color of the dirt on the ground.

EAT: Doves are ground feeders. They never land on a hanging feeder. They are gracious visitors and will eat almost any seed you have on the ground.

APPEARANCE: Unlike the blue jay, the dove is very shy and easily spooked, so they should be watched from a distance. They like to travel with a friend, so you will likely see more than one.

They more than likely get their name from the sad-sounding song they sing. You might think it sounds something like an owl's *who, who*. They don't sing all day like other outside birds. If you want to hear them, you must be quiet and patient. They will only talk when they think they are safe.

Doves love to sit around and watch the world go by. Sometimes, they even fall asleep sitting on a branch!

One word of warning: They will see you coming, but you may not see them. They use the element of surprise to their advantage. If you get too close for comfort, they will make noise and flap their wings wildly as they fly away!

RUBY-THROATED HUMMINGBIRD

COLOR: The handsome male has a shiny green body like the female, but he also has a bright red throat, which the female does not have. They are very small, no bigger than your hand. Their beak is very long and pointy.

EAT: This winged jewel doesn't eat seed at all. These birds prefer bugs and nectar from flowers. (Nectar is the sweet, sugary juice you find in certain flowers.) This doesn't mean you have to go buy flowers to attract hummers to your yard, although that would help. These little guys are not picky. You can buy hummingbird feeders at any store and fill them with a homemade sugary recipe (recipe in the back of this book), and you are set.

Did you know that they have a favorite color? They love red! So if you can plant red flowers or buy a red feeder, they will come sooner.

APPEARANCE: Rubies are the only species of hummers that live around us. They come to your yard from April until mid-September, depending on the temperature. They are very sensitive to the cold and choose to stay safe and warm rather than eat when it is chilly. They are able to go into what is called "torpor." This allows them to slow their heart rate and breathing, thereby saving energy to keep warm.

Hummingbirds are very good flyers and can fly forward and backward because of their unique wing design.

August is the best time to watch your hummers because they get very territorial. What that means is they pick a feeder and they call it theirs! They sit all day long and shoo away all the females and any males who come to drink.

Did I tell you how brave they are? They can be coaxed to drink out of your hand. Many people have said that, as they are filling their feeders, the hummers will fly all around their heads and drink while they are still filling it up!

Another great thing about these birds is how much they like family. If you faithfully feed your hummingbirds every year, they will bring their growing family, and in a few years you will have many more!

If you want to learn more about these awesome birds, there are several books at the library dedicated to just hummingbirds.

GRACKLES, RED-WINGED BLACKBIRDS, STARLINGS and CROWS

COLOR: Both the males and females are all black. The exception is the red-winged blackbird, whose male has an obvious red and yellow strip on its wing. The other would be the grackle, which is smaller than the others and has spots.

EAT: Unfortunately, these birds eat anything! The only feeder they won't invade is a thistle feeder, a favorite of the goldfinch.

APPEARANCE: These birds are no fun to have around! Farmers don't even like them! They frighten all the other birds away. They will eat everything you put out, much like ill-mannered pigs. They have even been known to break feeders in their feeding frenzy. They travel in packs and make a lot of unpleasant noise. You won't see much of them in the winter, but come spring and summer they are in abundance!

RED-BELLIED WOODPECKER

COLOR: The first thing you will notice on this interesting bird is the black-and-white, zebra-like print on its back. Both males and females have red on the top of the neck. The red on the male covers the whole top of his head, while the female has only a strip across the top. Both the male and female have white bellies.

EAT: Red-bellies love to munch on sunflower and suet cakes.

APPEARANCE: Like the nuthatch, they also grab their snack and fly to a quieter spot to enjoy it.

JUNCO "SNOWBIRDS"

COLOR: The male junco is a dark grey, but they may appear to be black or dark blue. He has white on his belly and on either side of his tail. The female is a lighter grey and is not as pretty.

EAT: Juncos, like sparrows, prefers to eat off the ground. Occasionally they will eat from a suet feeder.

APPEARANCE: Can you guess when you are most likely to see the most snowbirds? As their name indicates, these birds are most commonly seen when it's cold or snowy. They are such fun to watch when the snow has covered the ground. In an effort to try and scratch up seed that has been covered by snow, they hop and skid, hop and skid until they get to uncovered ground or unearth some fallen seed.

Although they are around in the summer, you won't likely see them at your backyard feeder.

HOUSE FINCH

COLOR: The male has brown stripes with a red belly and face. The female has no red at all.

EAT: House finches will eat any seed from any feeder, as well as seed on the ground.

APPEARANCE: These funny birds are very alert to what is happening around them. I think they watch more than they eat.

The finch family is large. There are several different kinds you may see in your backyard. The house finch is the most common. Of course, as you watch faithfully, you will definitely see others that I have not mentioned.

PILEATED WOODPECKER

COLOR: This spectacular bird has a large black body with a bright red fluff on the top of his head and a red mustache. The side of his face and neck carry a white stripe. The female is the same but with an all black mustache.

EAT: The pileated woodpecker eats the same as the red-bellied woodpecker.

APPEARANCE: These birds, compared to the others you will see in your yard, are enormous! It is much more difficult for them to eat at your feeder because they are so big. Other birds will usually wait patiently until the big guy has had his fill.

HOUSE SPARROW

COLOR: The male version of these little fellas have all brown bodies with a black patch on their throats and grey on the top of their heads. They also have a white stripe on their cheeks that you may or may not see from a distance. The female, who is not as pretty at all, is completely brown.

EAT: Sparrows will eat anything and anywhere! You may see them eyeballing your fries in a McDonald's parking lot or even cleaning up after you at your favorite amusement park or, yes, in your backyard. So these un-picky birds will eat any seed you give them.

APPEARANCE: This bird is probably familiar to everyone. Their shape and beak are identical to the goldfinch and several other species of birds found around the area. They are very content to feed on the ground, taking the seed no one else wants.

HOW TO WATCH THE
BIRDS IN YOUR YARD

I know how exciting it is to see such pretty birds flitting around in your very own backyard! The first thing we want to do is run over to them to get a closer look and try to strike up a conversation, but this is not the way to make feathered friends! As you learned from reading about your favorite birds, many of them are shy guys and don't like anyone to get too close. Also, certain times of the year they may be protecting their babies in a nearby nest. Birds are very protective of their young, just like your mom and dad are with you. So, as you watch the birds, keep a safe distance from wherever they are. This rule applies to any wild animal, anywhere you go. You might want to ask someone in your family to show you how to use binoculars. (Binoculars are a type of glasses you hold up to your face, allowing you to see farther away.)

With you watching from a distance, your birds will feel safe and will be sure to return. Also, when we let birds and animals behave without fear and don't interfere, they act naturally, so you may see some crazy things happen when they think no one is looking!

Next, it's important to watch birds in your yard quietly. *Shhh!* Don't yell to your mom or dad, "HEY! LOOK AT THE BEAUTIFUL GOLDFINCH!" You will be sure to scare the goldfinch and every other bird away. Instead, listen and let the birds talk and sing to you.

These bird-watching rules require *a lot* of patience! The reward will be worth it, I promise! I have had hummingbirds hover in front of my face and even had a finch land on my head!

WHAT DO MY BIRDS NEED?

O ne of the greatest things about having birds in your yard is they don't really need much. You can go crazy and have every kind of feeder made or you can have just one. If you are creative, find a pinecone and smear a mixture of peanut butter and mixed seed on the pinecone and hang it by a string from a tree.

You can also have a simple, multi-purpose bird feeder that dispenses mixed seed. These are available at just about any store, and both the feeder and seed are inexpensive. The downside to this feeder is some of the mixed seed is literally shoved out by the birds to get to the good sunflower seeds. That leaves 90 percent of the rest on the ground.

If you want to do it right, you will want to get yourself two different feeders. The first is a thistle feeder. It looks like a tube and, depending on its length, has several holes and perches. This feeder only holds nyger (thistle) seed. Finches of all kinds *love* this seed, and the doves can be found foraging the overspill. The second is a sunflower feeder. These come in every shape, color, and size. Many different birds will eat from your sunflower feeder. The downside is that squirrels love sunflower seed too. There are thousands of feeders, chemicals, contraptions, and home remedies to get rid of them, but I have not found anything foolproof. Those furry things are smart and hungry!

To attract woodpeckers you need a suet feeder. This feeder looks like a cage made of wire, and it holds pieces of fat or a square suet cake. The cakes are a combination of lard, seed, nuts, fruit, etc. Because of their content, the suet is best used in the winter. You may keep it filled all year, but it can become really messy in the heat of the summer. You can make these cakes yourself or, for under a dollar, you can go to the pet aisle of your supermarket and buy already-made cakes. This feeder will be worth the purchase because of the beautiful woodpeckers and nuthatches you will see. The ingredients in the cakes provide essentials that these birds need to give them energy through the winter.

We certainly couldn't leave out hummingbirds. The feeders for these guys are varied, and some are as beautiful as the bird itself. They come in every shape and size. You can get one to hang from a tree or suction to your window or to stick in your flowerpot. The nectar formula is simple. Take one cup of sugar and four cups of water. Combine the ingredients in a pot and bring to a boil for five minutes. (Always remember to have an adult present when you are working with a stove.) When cool you can feed the birds. There is no need to add food dye to your nectar, as experts think it might be harmful to the hummingbirds. Instead be sure to buy a colorful feeder or go to your local dollar store and buy some red silk flowers. Tie them to the

top of the feeder and, *voila*, you have a colorful nectar dispenser. It won't be long before those winged jewels pay you a visit. Be sure to put your hummingbird feeder out in early April and keep it up until late September.

The last thing you might want to have in your yard is a birdbath. Birds need to drink, and they need to groom and keep pruned in order to fly properly and prevent disease. Water is not always easy to find, so by having a bath for them you are meeting a need they have and getting a great show in return! They make a huge mess when they take a bath, and they dance all over the place. You will love it!

Finally, be sure to keep all your bird feeders and baths very clean, especially in the heat of the summer. Seed and water tend to get rotten quicker when it's hot outside.

Whatever small thing you do to attract birds to your yard will yield BIG benefits, so go out and share the yard with God's wonderful creation!